KT-484-555

ROMANS, CELTS & VIKINGS

ROMANS, CELTS
& VIKINGS

Philip Steele

MILES KELLY
PUBLISHING

First published in 2002 by Miles Kelly Publishing Ltd,
Bardfield Centre, Great Bardfield, Essex, CM7 4SL

Copyright © Miles Kelly Publishing 2002

All rights reserved. No part of this publication may be reproduced, stored
in a retrieval system, or transmitted by any means, electronic,
mechanical, photocopying, recording or otherwise, without the prior
permission of the copyright holder.

ISBN 1-84236-468-5

2 4 6 8 10 9 7 5 3

Some material in this book can also be found
in the *Encyclopedia of British History*

Editorial Director: Belinda Gallagher
Project Manager: Kate Miles
Art Director: Jo Brewer
Picture Researcher: Liberty Newton
Production Manager: Elizabeth Brunwin

Contact us by email: info@mileskelly.net
Website: www.mileskelly.net

Printed in China

CONTENTS

INTRODUCTION

This book takes us back to troubled days when the beaches and river valleys of Britain and Ireland were routes of invasion. Time after time between about 2,700 and 950 years ago, attackers, settlers and raiders arrived in the British Isles. They founded new kingdoms and brought with them new beliefs and technologies.

Our story begins with the Celts. These were iron-working peoples, whose culture spread far and wide across Europe. Celtic religious beliefs and ways of life readily took root in the islands, and were reinforced in places by invasion. The Celts of ancient Ireland were known as Gaels, while the Celts of ancient Britain were called Britons. The last Celtic invasion was by tribes known as Belgae, who settled in the southeast of Britain.

In 55BC these tribes were attacked by the Romans, whose Italian homeland was becoming the centre of a vast empire. In AD 43 the Romans returned to conquer much of Britain. They created a land of towns, temples, country estates, army camps and well-built roads. Their soldiers marched the length and breadth of Britain, but failed to hold the far north of the island. The Roman empire collapsed in the west in AD 476. Many of the Britons had by now adopted the Roman way of life, including a new faith called Christianity.

They were immediately under attack. Gaels raided the north and west, seizing land in western Scotland. Germanic peoples such as the Angles and Saxons crossed the North Sea.

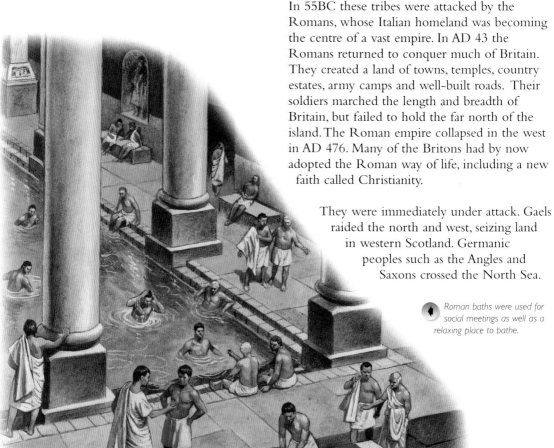

Roman baths were used for social meetings as well as a relaxing place to bathe.

By the late 700s and 800s all the peoples of the British Isles were under attack once again, from more Germanic raiders and invaders. These ones came from Scandinavia and were known as Northmen or Vikings. They came to rule large areas of the British Isles.

Historians used to call the period after the fall of Rome the 'Dark Ages'. However it was not just a time of gloom and doom and violence. Irish monks produced splendid works of art. This was an age of poetry, law-making and debate in many parts of the British Isles. It was an age in which England, Wales, Scotland and Ireland began to take shape. Many of the peoples who live in Britain and Ireland today are descended from the invaders and settlers of these exciting years.

Vikings or Northmen were medieval sea warriors. They invaded England and other European countries during the 8th - 11th centuries.

Over the centuries they pushed the Britons westwards and new Anglo-Saxon kingdoms were founded, in what became England. The Britons were eventually cut off in Cornwall and what became Wales, and in these areas Celtic kingdoms flourished.

Viking longships were shallow-draughted, narrow and very easy to manoeuvre at sea and up rivers.

ROMANS, CELTS & VIKINGS

THE WORLD AT A GLANCE

ELSEWHERE IN EUROPE

c700 BC
Rise of Celtic civilization in Central Europe

509 BC
Rome expels kings and becomes a republic

432 BC
The Parthenon temple is built in Athens, Greece

27 BC
Rome becomes an empire under the rule of Augustus

AD 410
Visigoth warriors sack the city of Rome

AD 476
End of the Roman empire in western Europe

AD 711
Moslem Moors (Arabs and Berbers) invade Spain from North Africa

AD 732
Charles Martel, ruler of the Franks, drives Arab invaders from France

AD 800
Charlemagne, ruler of the Franks, is crowned emperor in Rome

AD 962
King Otto I of Germany becomes Holy Roman Emperor

ASIA

c660 BC
Jimmu, legendary first emperor of Japan

c563 BC
Birth of religious teacher Gautama Siddhartha (the Buddha) in Nepal

550 BC
Cyrus the Great founds the Persian empire

334 BC
Alexander the Great begins the Greek invasion of Western Asia

322 BC
Mauryan empire is founded in India

cAD 30
Possible date for the crucifixion of Jesus Christ in Jerusalem

AD 132
Jews rebel against Roman rule and are scattered into exile

AD 552
The Buddhist faith reaches Japan from China

AD 570
Muhammad the Prophet, founder of Islam, is born in Mecca, Arabia

AD 802
The Angkor kingdom is founded by Khmer rulers in Cambdodia

AFRICA

c450 BC
Rise of Nok civilization in Nigeria, iron working, terracotta heads

c400 BC
Phoenician city of Carthage, North Africa, at height of power

331 BC
Greeks found city of Alexandria, Egypt

AD 44
Romans now rule North Africa from Egypt to Morocco

AD 50
Kingdom of Axum, in Ethiopia, rises to power

AD 429
The Vandals, a Germanic people, found kingdom in North Africa

AD 531
A Christian Church is founded in Ethiopia, North Africa

AD 600
Rise of the powerful gold-producing kingdom of Ghana, in West Africa

AD 750
Trade across the Sahara desert between North and West Africa

AD 969
Foundation of the city of Cairo, on the River Nile in Egypt

700BC–1066

Sutton Hoo helmet

NORTH AMERICA

c500 BC
Picture writing (hieroglyphs) at Monte Albán, Mexico

c310 BC
Chiefdoms in America's eastern woodlands - the Hopewell culture

c100 BC
The Hohokam people of the American South irrigate their crops

cAD 1
Possible date for first Arawak settlement of the Caribbean islands

cAD 50
The city of Teotihuacán is built in Mexico, massive pyramids

cAD 300
Height of the Maya civilization in Mexico, great cities

AD 800
The 'Dorset' culture amongst Inuit hunters of Canada and Greenland

AD 950
The Toltecs found the city of Tula in central Mexico

AD 1000
Vikings try to found settlements in Labrador and Newfoundland

AD 1050
The Anasazi build defensive settlements in the southwest

SOUTH AMERICA

c700 BC
Rise of the Parácas civilization in Peru

c200 BC
Rise of the Nazca civilization in Peru

c200 BC
Nazca people scratch ceremonial lines across the desert, Peru

c200 BC
Decline of the Chavín civilization

cAD 1
The Moche people of northern Peru, gold working and pottery

cAD 100
Growth of the city of Tiwanaku, near Lake Titicaca

cAD 400
Powerful chiefdom on Marajó island at mouth of the River Amazon

AD 700
The Andean city state of Wari becomes very powerful

AD 700
The decline of the Moche culture in northern Peru

AD 750
The Nazca civilization of southern Peru comes to an end

AD 900
The Chimú empire at the height of its power in northern Peru

OCEANIA

c300 BC
Polynesian settlement of Ellice Islands (Tuvalu)

c200 BC
Later burials at Aboriginal site of Roonka Flat, Australia

cAD 1
Large increase in the Aboriginal population of Australia

cAD 150
Egyptian geographer Ptolemy suggests 'unknown southern land' - perhaps Australia

cAD 400
Polynesians reach Easter Island, eastern South Pacific

cAD 400
Polynesians reach the Hawaiian Islands, Central Pacific

cAD 800
Earliest evidence for Polynesian hand clubs made of wood and whalebone

cAD 850
The Maoris, a Polynesian people, settle New Zealand coasts

cAD 1000
Last phase of Pacific settlement by Polynesian seafarers

cAD 1000
Easter Islanders begin to raise huge heads of carved stone

10

⊚⊚ c1500 BC
Iron working mastered in Western Asia. Skills spread east and west.

⊚⊚ c700 BC
Celtic tribes powerful in Central Europe

⊚⊚ c600 BC
Start of iron working in the British Isles

⊚⊚ c600 BC
Celts from Germany settle in northeast Scotland and spread north and west

⊚⊚ c400 BC
Iron now common throughout the British Isles

MASTERS OF IRON

THE CELTIC PEOPLES 1ST CENTURY BC

ALBION
OR ALBU
(GREAT BRITAIN)

Caledonians

Selgovae
Votadini
Venicones
Robogdi
Novantae
Erdini Darini
Nagnatae Voluntii
Auteni
Eblanii
Brigantes
NORTH SEA
Parisi
GAELS Cauci
BRITONS
Gangani Manapi
Deceangli Cornovii Coritani
Usdiae Coriondi IRISH Ordovices
Iceni
Iverni Brigantes SEA
Trinovantes
Vellabori
Demetae Catuvellauni
Dobunni
Silures
Atrebates Cantiaci
IERNE
OR ÉRIU
(IRELAND)
Durotriges
Dumnonii
ENGLISH CHANNEL

OPPER and bronze continued to be used for making all sorts of tools, weapons and jewellery, but soon a new metal was being worked in Europe. It was iron – so hard and tough that for centuries it was believed to be magical. Iron working was first mastered in western Asia, between 2000 and 1500 BC. By about 600 BC smiths were hammering out glowing bars of iron in the British Isles, too.

The British Celts, like the Gaels, formed many different tribes. Some were new invaders from the European mainland, others were native peoples who took up the Celtic way of life.

THE ANCIENT CELTS

One group of Europeans became expert at working the new metal, iron. The ancient Greeks called them 'Celts'. Their ancestry may have been the same as that of the Beaker People. The Celtic homeland was in Central Europe, southern Germany and the Alps, but after about 700 BC their influence spread across a vast area of Europe, from Turkey to Spain, from northern Italy through France to the British Isles. They raided and looted, they settled and farmed new lands. Trading and travel led to their way of life being adopted by other peoples, too. Northwest Europe was dominated by three main Celtic groups. Gauls lived in what is now France. Britons lived in Great Britain and Gaels lived in Ireland.

The Celts were brilliant metal workers who often decorated their work with birds, animals and interlacing patterns. Bronze mirrors like these were used after 100 BC by the Belgae, Celtic tribes who had settled in southern England.

◎◎ c350 BC	◎◎ c250 BC	◎◎ c150 BC	◎◎ c150 BC	◎◎ c100 BC	11
Celtic settlement of north and south of England, and Ireland	New waves of Celtic settlement in England, Scotland and Ireland	Fifteen Celtic tribes ('Belgae') invade England from Gaul	Celtic way of life at its greatest extent in Europe.	Celts increasingly under attack in mainland Europe	

CELTIC SOCIETY

The ancient Celts never saw themselves as one people and were rarely united. Celtic tribes were ruled by kings and by queens, too, for women held considerable power. Warriors came from noble families and prided themselves on being brave, heroic fighters and skilled hunters. They loved feasting and drinking. Both British and Gaelic tribes fought endlessly amongst themselves, quarrelling and raiding each others' cattle. The poorer members of the tribe were farmers, toiling on the land, raising animals and cutting the hay. They served as charioteers and fort-builders. Prisoners of war and lawbreakers were treated as slaves.

The ancient Celts were famed for their love of gold and jewellery. Nobles wore splendid brooches, rings, armbands and torcs (ornate metal collars).

This 2000 year-old iron chain was once fixed around the necks of slaves. It was found in a Welsh lake called Llyn Cerrig Bach, along with swords, spears, daggers, shields and chariots. They may have been thrown into the lake as offerings to the gods.

This ancient white horse design is carved into the chalk at Uffington, Oxfordshire, England. Its date is uncertain. By the Iron Age horses had become very important. The Celts mostly rode small, stocky ponies, but probably bred larger, more powerful horses too.

CELTIC LANGUAGES

Most of the languages spoken today in lands from Western Europe to northern India share a common origin. They are called Indo-European. Some languages still spoken in modern times came down to us from the ancient Celts. The language of the Britons turned into Welsh, Cornish and Breton (spoken in Brittany, France). The language of the Gaels gave us Irish, Scottish Gaelic and Manx (spoken on the Isle of Man). In Britain, no fewer than six rivers are called Avon. Why? It is simply a Celtic word for 'river'.

12

◎◎ c600 BC
First settlement at Colchester, Essex England

◎◎ c450 BC
A flourishing of Celtic arts and crafts across Europe.

◎◎ c325 BC
First documented reference to the name British ('Pretanic') Isles

◎◎ c300 BC
According to legend, a hospital is founded in Armagh, Ireland

◎◎ c200 BC
Fortified mountain settlement of Tre'r Ceiri, Llŷn peninsula, Wales

FORTS HAD been built in the British Isles before the Iron Age. They were large enclosures protected by earthworks and walls, and were sited on hilltops and headlands. They often enclosed dwellings which were occupied in peacetime as well as war. New enclosures were raised by the Celts. Within Tre'r Ceiri hillfort, on a misty mountain side in North Wales, the stone walls of 150 huts built in about 200 BC can still be seen today. Farming villages often had to be built on less protected lowlands, wherever the soil was good. In Ireland and Scotland, some villages were built on crannogs, artifical islands in lakes. The last of the Celtic invaders, the Belgae, built sizeable towns, such as St Albans and Colchester.

Inside the Celtic roundhouse, smoke drifted up to the rafters from the central hearth, and left through a hole in the roof. The timber posts may have been carved with ornate decorations. People slept on the ground in the cubicles, beneath warm animal skins.

THE CELTS AT HOME

ROUND HOUSES

Royal enclosures may have included large, rectangular halls, but most ordinary people in the western lands of the Celts lived in large round huts, which measured about 15 metres across. The roofs were cone-shaped with a heavy thatch. The walls were normally built of timber and wattle-and-daub (interlaced sticks covered in clay). Stone was used in areas where timber was scarce.

On the floor
Floors were of beaten earth or slabs. They could be strewn with sweet-smelling rushes or grasses.

The hearth
A wood fire in the centre of the hut was used for cooking and heating.

◎◎ c100 BC	◎◎ c100 BC	◎◎ c90 BC	◎◎ c75 BC	◎◎ c75 BC	13
Lake village at Glastonbury, Somerset, England	Beautifully decorated hand mirrors become popular	First British coins, southern England	Thriving trade between Britain and Gaul	Large towns grow up in the lands occupied by Belgic Celts	

A LOVE OF FINERY

Celtic women wore long, loose dresses and tunics made of wool or linen, and wore shawls and cloaks fastened by brooches and pins. Men wore short tunics, cloaks and – a new fashion copied from the horse-riding warriors of Eastern Europe and Asia – trousers. Cloth was coloured with vegetable dyes and checked patterns were popular. Hair was often worn long and men favoured large, drooping moustaches. Both sexes loved to wear jewellery.

 *A modern weaver recreates the Iron Age way of weaving. She passes a shuttle with yarn through the upright threads, which are stretched on an upright loom.*

Livestock
Farm animals were kept in pens or even in the same huts as the villagers. They included sheep, goats, pigs, cattle and horses.

The loom
Looms (weaving frames) stood in most huts, for each household would produce its own cloth.

The Iron Age diet was quite healthy. The Celts kept bees and honey was used to sweeten food and drink in the days before sugar was known in Europe.

Compartments
Each hut was really one single room, but the inside edge of the wall was divided into separate cubicles, used for storage of weapons and supplies or for sleeping.

WHAT'S FOR DINNER?
A big cauldron steamed over each hearth and the Celts were famous for enjoying their food. They might eat beef, mutton or pork, cheese or buttermilk. Bread and porridge were made from wheat, barley, rye or oats. Hunting and fishing provided boar, venison (deer meat) or salmon. Southern Europeans were amazed by the large amounts of alcohol drunk by Celtic men and women – imported wine, home-brewed ale and mead, a drink made from honey.

apples

wild boar

honey

nuts

c700 BC
Royal fort of Emain Macha,
northern Ireland

c450 BC
First Iron Age phase of
Maiden Castle, Dorset,
England

c450 BC
South Barrule hillfort,
Isle of Man

c300 BC
Celts in mainland Europe
probably invent chain mail

c250 BC
War chariots introduced to
the British Isles

WARRIOR HEROES

THE CELTS were famed as fighters through most of Europe. Far to the south of the British Isles, Celtic warrior bands were storming into Rome and Greece between 387 BC and 279 BC. Celtic tribes did take part in large pitched battles, but they preferred single combat, where champions from each army came out to fight each other. They belonged to an age which admired individual bravery more than organization or discipline. In the royal halls, warriors would boast of their exploits and drink to their dead companions.

Maiden Castle in Dorset, England, was already an important site during the New Stone Age. From about 450 BC, it was a major hillfort and the capital of a Celtic tribe called the Durotriges.

Timber defences
Heavy timbers were used to build fences and gates, the last line of defence against invaders.

High earthworks
The banks were staggered so that it was impossible to launch a direct attack on the gates. The fort was finally taken by the Romans.

The settlement
The settled area covered 18 hectares. Finds here have included Iron Age pots, sickles, combs made of bone and the skeletons of warriors who died in battle.

RATHS, DUNS AND BROCHS

Some forts were large defended settlements, but others were smaller and built more like castles. The remains of stone 'duns' may still be seen in Scotland and royal 'raths' in Ireland. The Picts, ancient inhabitants of northeastern Scotland who adopted the Celtic way of life, built 'brochs' – big stone towers which could be used as shelter in wartime.

A charioteer races his horses outside the dun, always ready for war.

CELTIC CHARIOTS

A new wave of Celtic warriors reached the British Isles in about 250 BC. With them came the light war chariot. Built of wood, it had iron-rimmed wheels and was pulled by two tough ponies, bred for their speed. It was driven by a non-fighting charioteer and was used to carry a fully armed warrior into battle. Some warriors who died were buried in their chariots.

◎◎ c120 BC
Celtic sword blades at their longest, up to 90 cm

◎◎ c100 BC
Southern English hillforts strengthened against attacks by the Belgae

◎◎ c30 BC
Possible date of a ceremonial horned helmet found in the River Thames

◎◎ c1 BC
Broch built on Mousa, Shetland Isles

◎◎ cAD 20
Possible date of bronze ceremonial shields discovered in Britain

15

CÚ CHULAINN, CHAMPION OF THE GAELS?

Some tales told by the ancient Celts were written down many centuries later, during the Middle Ages. The Irish tales tell of Sétanta, nick-named Cú Chulainn ('the Hound of Culain'), a legendary hero of Ulster in northern Ireland. As a boy he kills a fierce hound. As a youth he is trained in fighting by a female warrior called Scáthach. He has a magic spear and as a man takes on the invading army of Queen Medb of Connaught single-handed. Cú Chulainn represents everything the Celtic warrior wished to be. He is a cattle-raider, a warrior and a champion – swift, cunning, tireless and brave.

WEAPONS AND WARRIORS

Most Celts went into battle unprotected by helmets or armour. They often fought without any clothes at all, preferring to strip naked. Later, Celts on the European mainland did design very effective armour to use against the Romans. They may even have been the inventors of chain mail, armour made from linked rings of iron. Celtic warriors carried mostly long- or oval-shaped shields, spears, daggers and long slashing swords made of iron. Hillforts were defended with a hail of pebbles hurled from slings. Some Celtic warriors used lime to dress their hair into spikes and tattooed their skin with a blue dye, called woad – the name 'Picts' comes from the Latin for 'painted people'.

The Celtic warrior could use throwing spears and stabbing spears. His deadliest weapon was his long sword, which he whirled around his head and brought crashing down on the enemy.

16

ℭℭ **55 BC**
The first Roman invasion of
Great Britain

ℭℭ **54 BC**
The second Roman invasion
of Great Britain

ℭℭ **AD 9**
Cunobelinus becomes
king of the Catuvellauni

ℭℭ **AD 41**
Planned Roman invasion
fails to take place

ℭℭ **AD 43**
The start of the
final Roman conquest

ROMAN INVASION

AFTER ABOUT 100 BC, the Celts in mainland Europe came under attack from German and Central European warriors. From Italy, too, Roman armies marched northwards to conquer the Gauls. In August 55 BC the Roman general Julius Caesar landed near Deal, in Kent, with 10,000 troops. He met with furious resistance, but returned the following year with at least 30,000 foot soldiers and 2000 cavalry. This time they crossed the River Thames and invaded the tribal lands of the Catuvellauni, Belgic Celts who had settled around St Albans. The Britons of southeast England were forced to pay tribute to Rome and Caesar withdrew.

JULIUS CAESAR

The conqueror of the Gauls and southern Britons was one of the most brilliant generals the world has known. Born in about 100 BC, his military campaigns made him the most powerful man in Rome. He made many enemies and was stabbed to death in 44 BC.

Gaius Julius Caesar

The Roman invasion of AD 43 brought Britain into a vast empire, which stretched from Spain into Western Asia, and southwards into North Africa. Its capital was Rome. Britain marked the northern limits of Roman rule. The Romans never conquered the far north of Scotland and Ireland too remained free.

THE ROMANS RETURN

After the second Roman invasion, the Catuvellauni grew more powerful. Their new king, Cunobelinus, conquered neighbouring tribes. When he died in AD 43, these tribes joined with an exiled son of the king to ask the Romans if they would curb the power of the Catuvellauni. They did more than that. The emperor Claudius ordered a full-scale invasion of Britain.

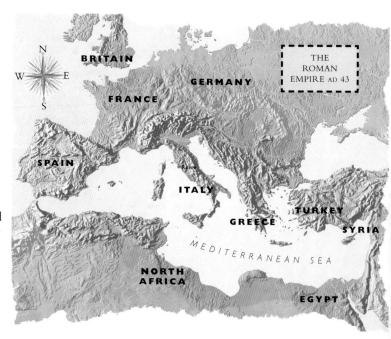

AD 48
Caratacus leads resistance of the British Celts

AD 51
Caratacus taken to Rome as a prisoner

AD 61
Boudicca sacks Colchester, St Albans and London

AD 70
The Romans attack the Brigantes tribe in Yorkshire

AD 84
The Romans defeat the Caledonian tribes at Mons Graupius

17

THE CONQUEST OF BRITAIN

The new invaders numbered about 40,000 Roman troops and auxiliaries – units called in from other parts of the empire. They fought their way through Kent, crossed the Thames and captured Colchester. There were savage battles at hillforts such as Maiden Castle. It took four years for the Romans to take control of southern Britain, and over 30 more to conquer Wales and the West.

CARATACUS THE REBEL

Eleven British rulers immediately allied themselves with the Roman invaders. However Caratacus or Caradoc, a son of Cunobelinus, waged a fierce guerrilla campaign. Defeated, he sought refuge with Cartimandua, queen of the Brigantes, but she handed him over to the Romans. He was taken to Rome in chains, but in the end was pardoned. He died in AD 52.

A LONG STRUGGLE

In AD 60 a bloody rising began in what is now East Anglia. The queen of the Iceni, Boudicca, burned down Colchester, St Albans and the new town of London. She was defeated the following year and committed suicide. By the 70s, the Romans had advanced into northern England. In AD 84 they defeated the massed tribes of southern Scotland at Mons Graupius, near Inverurie. Calgacus, the defeated leader, said bitterly: 'They make a wilderness and call it peace.'

Boudicca was the wife of Prasutagus, king of the Iceni. He made a treaty with the Romans, but when he died they seized his lands and assaulted his family. This sparked off the great rebellion of AD 60-61.

In AD 122 building work started on Hadrian's Wall, a line of defences and forts 115 kilometres long. It ran from the Solway Firth to the River Tyne. The wall was more of a communications and trading network than a final frontier.

18

⊙⊙ **AD 44**
Romans capture Maiden
Castle

⊙⊙ **AD 50**
Camolodunum (Colchester)
is centre of military command

⊙⊙ **AD 74**
Roman fort built at Isca
Silurum (Caerleon)

⊙⊙ **AD 75**
Roman fort begun at
Segontium (Caernarfon)

⊙⊙ **AD 79**
Deva (Chester) a major
Roman army base

THE IRON LEGIONS

I T TOOK the Roman troops many years to gain
control of the lands now known as England and Wales
and they failed to hold Scotland. In AD 118, 34 years
after the battle of Mons Graupius, a whole Roman legion
– the Ninth – marched north and was never seen again.
Hadrian's Wall was built in AD 122 to keep out the Picts
and other northern tribes and this became the frontier of
the empire. In AD 142 more northerly defences were
raised along the River Clyde and beyond, but a second
'Antonine' Wall soon had to be abandoned. Ireland
remained unconquered.

**BRITANNIA
(GREAT BRITAIN)**

Mare
Hibjerniae
(Irish Sea)

ROMAN
BRITAIN

Mare
Orientale
(North Sea)

Luguvalium
Carlisle

Eboracum
York

Segontium
Caernarfon

Deva
Chester

Lindum
Lincoln

Ratae
Leicester

Camoludunum
Colchester

Glevum
Gloucester

Verulamium
St Albans

Isca Silurum
Caerleon

Londinium
London

Venta Belgarum
Winchester

Dubris
Dover

Isca Dumnoniorum
Exeter

Mare Austrum
(English Channel)

⬤ The new Roman province
was called Britannia. London
soon outgrew Colchester as the
most important town. Important
bases for the legions were built at
Chester and York in northern
England and Caerleon in South
Wales. After about AD 213
Britannia was divided into two
regions – Upper and Lower.

THE ROMAN ARMY

Celts and Romans were very different
fighters. The Britons fought as heroic
individuals, the Romans as a ruthless
war machine. The Roman troops were
heavily armed and strictly disciplined.
They were organized into units called
legions, each with an eagle-headed
standard. At the time of the British
conquest each numbered about 5500
troops. Each legion was divided into
ten sections called cohorts and had
59 middle-ranking officers
called centurions.

⬤ Horses were used by
officers and by separate
cavalry units. These were armed
with long swords and spears.

⬤ When storming a hill fort,
Roman soldiers would
form a close unit, crouching with
shields covering their heads and
their sides. This formation was
called a testudo or tortoise.
Hillforts were also attacked with
huge catapults.

◎◎ AD 118	◎◎ AD 122	◎◎ AD 142	◎◎ AD 196	◎◎ AD 208	19
The Ninth Legion disappears in Scotland	Work begins on Hadrian's Wall	Building of the Antonine Wall in Scotland	Northern frontiers are overrun by British tribes	Romans try again to conquer Scotland, under Emperor Septimius Severus	

Throwing spear
The legionary's spear was a weighted javelin, made of wood and iron.

Hand-fighting
The legionary carried a short sword in a scabbard and also a dagger.

Armour
Caesar's legions wore armour of mail, but by the time of Claudius, Roman foot soldiers wore armour made of metal plates.

Sandals
Sandals were made from leather and the soles were studded iron for the long marches.

LETTERS FROM THE WALL
Life on Hadrian's Wall was hard for the Roman legionaries and the foreign auxiliaries stationed there. Winters were cold, duties were dull or sometimes dangerous, always exhausting. Archaeologists have found orders for supplies, accounts, requests for leave, and even letters from home saying that the underpants and socks requested have been sent.

Marching baggage
The legionary marched with a heavy bundle slung over his shoulder. It included all sorts of digging tools, buckets and clattering tins as well as his basic food rations – biscuits, cheese and bacon.

Shield
Roman shields at this time were rectangular. They were made of wood, leather and linen, with a boss (central stud) of iron or bronze.

The Roman legionary was soldier, builder, engineer and labourer all in one.

A SOLDIER'S LIFE

The Roman legionary was a paid, professional soldier. Recruits were given very hard training. They learned parade-ground drill and battle formations. They were forced to march very long distances. They were taught how to fight with swords and throw javelins, how to pitch camp and dig defences. Punishments for disobedience were harsh. At the time of the conquest of Britain, legionaries were not allowed to marry whilst in service. After 25 years, however, they could retire. Many then settled around military camps and towns, often marrying a British woman and raising a family.

AD 75
A splendid palace is built at Fishbourne, near Chichester, England

AD 78
Aquae Sulis (Bath) already famous for its warm springs

AD 90
A Roman theatre is built at Canterbury, Kent

c AD 90
Large town houses being built in Britain for the first time

AD 100
A Roman villa is built at Lullingstone, Kent, southern England

ROMAN PEACE

BRITISH REBELS were sold into slavery, but local rulers and nobles who supported Rome prospered. Many of them adopted Roman ways and dress. They learned to speak Latin, the language of Rome. Roman rule was often harsh, but it did bring a period of peace to large areas of Europe.

BRITISH AND ROMAN

Romans who stayed in Britain for more than a few years were influenced in turn by the Celts. Although Romans worshipped their own gods and goddesses, they were also prepared to honour many of the Celtic gods. When the Romans built luxurious new public baths at Bath, in western England, these were dedicated both to the Celtic goddess Sulis and the Roman goddess Minerva.

Gardens
Walkways with columns and statues passed through gardens of shrubs, herbs and fruit trees

The most impressive Roman villas were built in the AD 200s and 300s.

The hot springs at Bath, or Aquae Sulis, were believed to cure illnesses and injuries. The baths built there by the Romans attracted visitors from all over the empire.

ROMAN CRAFTS
British craft workers gradually learned to copy Roman skills such as making mosaics. These pictures, made from chips of coloured tile, decorated the floors of public buildings and the homes of the wealthy.

Mosaic from Fishbourne Palace, near Chichester, England

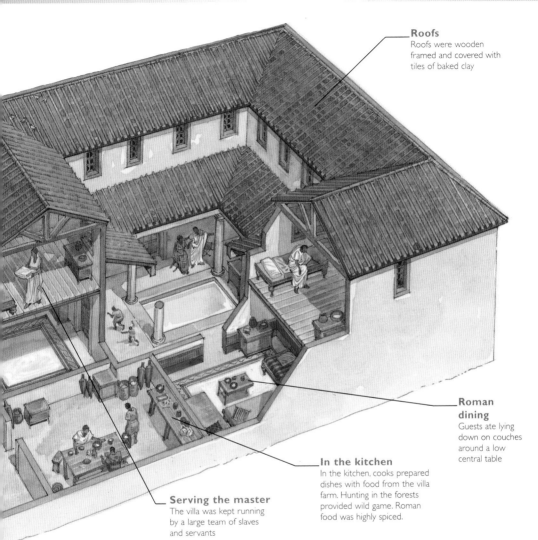

Roofs
Roofs were wooden framed and covered with tiles of baked clay

Roman dining
Guests ate lying down on couches around a low central table

In the kitchen
In the kitchen, cooks prepared dishes with food from the villa farm. Hunting in the forests provided wild game. Roman food was highly spiced.

Serving the master
The villa was kept running by a large team of slaves and servants

LIVING IN STYLE

Large country houses called villas were built for important Roman officials or for local British rulers who remained loyal to Rome. They were surrounded by large farm estates. Over the years, villas became more and more luxurious, with under-floor central heating, baths and dining rooms where visitors from Rome would be entertained with lavish banquets.

GODS FROM AFAR
New forms of worship arrived in Britain from distant lands. Mithras, the Persian god of light, was especially popular with the legions.

Mithras slays a bull

22

◎◎ AD 280
Start of Saxon raids on
southern and eastern Britain

◎◎ AD 287
Carausius rules Britain
independently

◎◎ AD 297
Rule from Rome is
restored in Britain

◎◎ AD 306
Constantine the Great is
declared Roman emperor
at York

◎◎ AD 360
The Mildenhall treasure is
buried in Suffolk

THE MIGHTY empire of Rome began to look less powerful after AD 200. There were bitter civil wars and struggles for power. In AD 286 the empire was divided into an eastern and western part. Britain was in the west, still ruled from Rome. However in AD 287 Carausius, commander of the Roman fleet in Britain, declared himself ruler of Britain. He was murdered by a fellow rebel, Allectus, in AD 293. Rome regained control in AD 297, but not for long. Frontier defences were now being breached all around the empire.

MAGNUS MAXIMUS

Magnus Maximus was a Spanish-born commander of the Roman troops in Britain. He made treaties with Celtic peoples such as the Votadini and Dumnonii to take on defending Britain against the Picts and Gaels. In AD 383 he marched with his troops to Rome and seized the throne. He was killed five years later. His memory survives in the folklore of Wales, where he is known as Macsen.

THE FALL OF ROME

INVADERS CHALLENGE ROME

Roman Britain now came under attack from all sides. In the far north the Picts overran Hadrian's Wall and advanced south. Western shores and shipping were under attack from the Gaels, the unconquered Celts of Ireland. The English Channel was plagued by pirates. Southern England and East Anglia were attacked by a people from Germany, the Saxons. From about AD 280 Romans built a chain of massive stone forts to defend southeastern coasts, which became known as the Saxon Shore.

A beacon blazes on top of a lighthouse as Roman ships patrol the English Channel. By AD 401 the legions were sailing away from Britain.

THE MILDENHALL TREASURE

In 1946 it was officially reported that four years earlier a Roman treasure hoard had been ploughed up at Mildenhall in Suffolk, England.

The pieces discovered were made of solid silver and dated from about AD 350. They may have originally been imported from Roman North Africa. They included spoons, splendid dishes, plates and wine goblets – 34 pieces in all.

In the days before banks and safes, people stored their wealth as precious metals. In times of war they would bury them at a secret spot, to prevent them falling into enemy hands. Hoards like this one suggest that by the 300s, Roman Britain was no longer a peaceful or secure place to live.

The frieze
A picture strip around the cover of the dish features lions, boars and centaurs – strange creatures which are half-human, half-horse.

Decorated silver
Although the spoons in the treasure hoard had early Christian emblems on them, this fine dish is decorated with pictures of non-Christian gods.

This splendid dish from the Mildenhall treasure hoard is now in the British Museum, in London.

END OF THE EMPIRE

Between AD 401 and 410, Roman troops were withdrawn from Britain as Germanic tribes crossed the River Rhine and poured into Gaul. Within the empire there were revolts and uprisings, and more attempts to seize local power. The economy collapsed. In AD 410 Rome itself was sacked by northern invaders called Goths. The emperor Honorius declared that from now on, the Britons would have to defend themselves. In AD 446 British leaders made one last appeal to Rome, but it was hopeless. It took just 30 more years for the Roman empire in Western Europe to come to an end.

The rim
The rim of the dish is finely patterned. None of the items were scratched or damaged by the plough.

24

🌸 **AD 430**
Possible date for rule of Ambrosius (Emrys) over Britons

🌸 **AD 448**
Vortigern asks Hengist and Horsa to help him fight the Picts

🌸 **AD 455**
Hengist and Horsa attack Vortigern. Horsa is killed

🌸 **AD 456**
Hengist and his son Aesc defeat Britons in Kent

🌸 **AD 477**
A Saxon war leader called Aelle lands at Selsey and invades Sussex

THE AGE ⊙F ARTHUR

THE thousand years between the fall of Rome and the start of modern European history are known as the Middle Ages. After Rome withdrew from Britain, the country was divided between local rulers. Many of them still tried to follow the Roman – and Christian – way of life. However trade was disrupted by war and grass grew through cracked pavements as Roman towns and villas fell into disrepair.

Dragons were used as emblems by the Britons after the Roman withdrawal. Dragons, originally an Asian design, were used on some Roman cavalry standards and may have appeared on the standard of Magnus Maximus. A red dragon remains the emblem of Wales today.

WHO WAS ARTHUR?

It cannot be proved that Arthur or Artorius, one of the most famous names in British history, existed at all. However many clues suggest that he was indeed a historical figure. If so, he was probably of noble birth, a British Celt and a Christian who followed the Roman way of life.

Arthur would have been a war leader or general rather than a king. He would have led a band of armoured, mounted warriors which could assist local defence groups, moving at speed to meet invading Saxons or Picts. He is linked with a great victory at somewhere called Mount Badon in about AD 516 and is said to have been killed at the battle of Camlan in AD 537.

During the later Middle Ages, tales about Arthur spread far and wide. Many of them mixed him up with ancient Celtic gods and heroes. He became a king in shining armour, famous for his bravery. Stories about Arthur and his companions were told in France, Germany and Italy.

Legend has it that Arthur was born at Tintagel, on the northern coast of Cornwall. This cliff-top site was inhabited in Roman times and by AD 500 had a Christian monastery. It also has the ruins of a castle from 500 years later.

❋ AD 495
Saxons under Cerdic invade Wessex (central Southern England)

❋ AD 516
Possible date for Battle of Mount Badon. Britons halt West Saxon advance

❋ AD 530
Saxons take the Isle of Wight

❋ AD 539
Supposed date for battle of Camlan and death of Arthur

❋ AD 547
Ida founds the Saxon kingdom of Bernicia at Bamburgh, Northumberland

25

NORTH SEA INVADERS

In eastern Britain there had been small settlements of retired auxiliaries from Germany since Roman times. Now roving Germanic warrior bands arrived across the North Sea. They were Angles, Saxons, Frisians and Jutes. They raided southern and eastern England and then seized the land. Their conflict with the Britons would last hundreds of years.

The British probably used small bands of cavalry to pursue the Saxon armies. They did slow down the Saxon advance, but they could not stop it.

ANCIENT TALES

The first mention of Arthur in literature comes in a series of fantastic tales, which were written down in Wales later in the Middle Ages. They had been passed down over the ages by word of mouth. Some are tales of ancient Celtic gods and the underworld, of severed heads and magical animals. Others refer to Magnus Maximus (Macsen), the age of Arthur and the Christian period. Today this group of tales is known as the *Mabinogion*.

BATTLING FOR BRITAIN

We know little of the kings and armies who defended Britain against the new invaders. Emrys or Ambrosius seems to have been a very powerful ruler in about AD 430, possibly later. In AD 449 another king called Vortigern invited two Jutes called Hengist and Horsa to help him fight the Picts, in return for land.

By AD 455 they had turned against Vortigern and were waging war on the Britons.

26

⚜ **AD 559**
Glappa becomes king of
Bernicia (Northumbria)

⚜ **AD 560**
King Ceawlin drives the
Britons from Wessex

⚜ **AD 560**
Ethelbert becomes king
of Kent

⚜ **AD 604**
Earliest record of a Saxon
land charter

⚜ **AD 644**
Northumbria is made up of
Deira and Bernicia

SAXON SWORDS

THE invasion of southern and eastern Britain by Angles, Saxons, Frisians and Jutes was just one part of a great movement of Germanic peoples across Europe. German lands in Central Europe were being invaded by fierce warriors from the east, such as the Huns and the Slavs. The Germanic peoples who lived there looked westwards at the crumbling defences of the old Roman empire. There they saw rich farmland for the taking and a chance to carve out new kingdoms for themselves. Germanic tribes poured into France, Italy, Spain and North Africa.

CELTS AND SAXONS

The Britons believed that the Angles and Saxons were savages. These peoples had never experienced the civilisation of Rome, nor were they Christians. In reality, however, the Germanic invaders were not so different from the British Celts. They shared similar European origins and lived in small kingdoms. They depended on farming and fishing. They shared the same technology and were fine craft workers.

THE DAY OF WODEN
The newcomers brought with them worship of the ancient Germanic gods. These survive in English names for days of the week. Tuesday is named after Tiw, god of war. Wednesday is the day of Woden, the chief god. Thursday is the day of Thor, god of thunder. Friday is from Frigg, goddess of love.

Woden, also known as Wotan or Odin

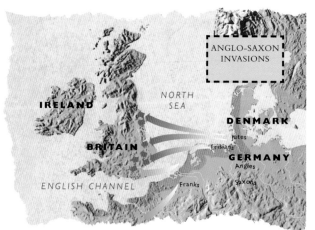

The invaders came from the lands now occupied by Germany, Denmark and the Netherlands. They crossed the North Sea and English Channel in wooden boats and fought their way westwards.

THATCH AND TIMBER
The various Germanic invaders can be grouped together under the general name 'Anglo-Saxons'. It was their language which eventually became English. They built small farming villages, many of whose names survive as English place names today. Their houses were rectangular, with walls of timber planks and pitched roofs covered in a heavy thatch. These were surrounded by a fenced yard. In some regions, huts seem to have been raised over sunken pits, which may have been boarded over.

❋ AD 625	❋ AD 625	❋ AD 642	❋ AD 655	❋ AD 668	27
Probable date of the Sutton Hoo burial in East Anglia	First Anglo-Saxon coins to be minted in England	Penda of Mercia kills Oswald of Northumbria at Maserfeld	Penda of Mercia killed by Oswiu of Northumbria at Battle of the Winwaed	Ine becomes king of Wessex, first records of Anglo-Saxon laws	

ANGLO-SAXON LANDS

Modern names for counties and regions of England recall the first advances of the Anglo-Saxons. Essex comes from East Seaxe, land of the East Saxons. Sussex come from Suth Seaxe, land of the South Saxons. East Anglia was East Engle, the eastern territory of the Angles. By AD 550 the Anglo-Saxons controlled large areas of eastern and southern Britain. The Britons still ruled in the west and much of the north.

Anglo-Saxon warriors of the AD 400s and 500s might be armed with a battle axe, a long sword, a spear, or a long knife called a sax. They wore woollen tunics over trousers and carried round shields. Chieftains wore helmets and shirts of mail.

A ROYAL SHIP BURIAL

In 1939 a grave was discovered at Sutton Hoo, near Woodbridge in Suffolk, England. It was a royal burial, probably that of Raedwald, a ruler of East Anglia who died in about AD 625. He was buried in a ship beneath a mound of earth. His ship was 27 metres long and was rowed by 40 oars. Inside a wooden chamber in the boat was a rich treasure hoard. There were buckles and fasteners of shining gold, a jewel-covered purse containing 37 gold coins. There was a musical instrument called a lyre. There was a sword, a shield and the remains of a splendid helmet made of iron and bronze.

The ornate Sutton Hoo helmet shows the influence of Roman styles on European design 200 years after the collapse of the Roman empire.

28

✸ CAD 500
The founding of the kingdom
of Dál Riada by Fergus Mór

✸ AD 574
Colmcille crowns Aedán
MacGabráin High King
of Dál Riada

✸ AD 604
Strathclyde and Dál
Riada defeated by Angles
at Degsástan

✸ AD 642
Owain of Strathclyde defeats
Dál Riada at Strathcarron

✸ CAD 650
Dál Riada loses its territories
in northern Ireland

THE MAKING OF SCOTLAND

S COTLAND takes its name from a people whom the Romans called Scoti. These 'Scots' were Gaels who sailed from northern Ireland to raid Britain's western coasts and islands as the Roman empire collapsed. By AD 500 they had founded a kingdom called Dál Riada on the Scottish mainland. For many years the Scots battled with the Picts, who still controlled the lands of the northeast, around Aberdeen. The monk Colmcille (Columba) was an Irish-born Scot, and he hoped that once these northern Picts had become Christian, the two peoples could live in peace.

BATTLE FOR THE LOWLANDS

Picts were one of four groups of people living in Scotland at this time.

The Angles who had founded Bernicia (later part of Northumbria) soon pushed further northwards, into the Scottish Lowlands. The Britons living in the Lowlands were under pressure from all sides. They made an alliance with the Scots to fight the Angles, but were defeated at the battle of Degsástan (perhaps near Jedburgh) in AD 603. The Angles now controlled the Lothian region – eastern Scotland below the Firth of Forth. This left the Britons of the Lowlands isolated in their kingdom of Strathclyde. Their lands to the south were also being overrun by Angles and they were soon cut off from their fellow Britons in Wales.

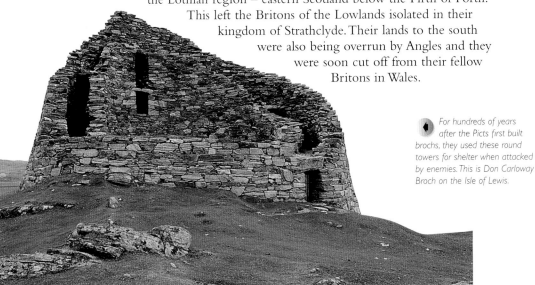

For hundreds of years after the Picts first built brochs, they used these round towers for shelter when attacked by enemies. This is Don Carloway Broch on the Isle of Lewis.

❄ **AD 685**
Picts stop northern advance of Angles at Nechtansmere

❄ **AD 736**
Victories of Picts under King Óengus I against Scots of Dál Riada

❄ **AD 768**
King Áed Find of Dál Raida invades Pictish kingdom of Fortriu

❄ **AD 841**
Kenneth I MacAlpin becomes King of Dál Riada

❄ **AD 843**
Scots and Picts unite in Kingdom of Alba

29

This beautiful wooden box, the Monymusk Reliquary, is decorated with gilt and silver. It was made in the 600s or 700s and is said to have contained the remains of Colmcille (Columba).

DÁL RIADA

The new kingdom of Dál Riada included part of northern Ireland, islands such as Iona, and the Argyll region of the Scottish mainland. By about AD 650 the Scots had lost their lands back in Ireland. Cut off from their homeland, the dialect of Irish that they spoke gradually developed into the Gaelic language still spoken today in the islands and highlands of Scotland.

Kenneth I succeeded his father Alpin as King of the Scots in AD 841. Two years later he united the lands of the Scots and the Picts. He died in AD 858.

THE KINGDOM OF ALBA

In AD 685 the Picts halted the northward advance of the Angles with a desperate battle at Nechtansmere, Dunnichen. But it was not until AD 843 that northern Scotland finally became united. That was when a ruler of the Scots called Kenneth MacAlpin ('mac' meaning 'son of') joined his kingdom with that of the Picts.

The centre of the Christian Church in Scotland now moved eastwards from Iona to Dunkeld, in Perthshire. The new kingdom was called Alba and it linked up most of the region lying to the north of the Firth of Forth and the River Clyde.

It was one of the most important kingdoms in the Celtic world and formed the chief building block of the future kingdom of Scotland. Alba rarely knew peace, for it was under constant attack by Anglo-Saxons from the south and by Scandinavians around its coasts.

THE STONE OF DESTINY

A ceremonial slab of sandstone was brought by the Scots from Ireland to Iona. From there it was taken to Dunstaffinage and later to Scone, near Perth. This 'Stone of Destiny' was used at the coronation of the kings of Alba and of united Scotland. In 1297 the English King Edward I stole the stone and took it south to London. There it stayed until 1950, when it was reclaimed by four Scottish students. The stone was recovered in Arbroath and returned to England. However in 1996 it was officially installed in Edinburgh Castle.

⚜ **CAD 540**
The voyages of Brendan around North Atlantic coasts

⚜ **CAD 550**
Start of the age of the monasteries in Ireland

⚜ **AD 561**
Brendan founds Clonfert monastery, Galway

⚜ **CAD 600**
Ogham script now replaced by the Roman alphabet

⚜ **CAD 600**
The royal house of Uí Néill becomes the most powerful in Ireland

A LIGHT IN IRELAND

HISTORIANS used to call the period after the fall of Rome the 'Dark Ages', because European civilization was torn apart by war. However the darkness did not cover all of Europe. Ireland, in the far northwest, was a shining example. It had escaped Roman rule and trade now prospered with Cornwall, Brittany and southwestern Europe. Between about AD 700 and 800, Celtic arts and crafts reached the high point in their history.

The Tara brooch is made of gilded bronze and silver and is decorated with glass and amber. It probably dates from about AD 700.

ART OF THE MONKS

Christian monasteries in Ireland became great centres of learning. They also held great political influence. Important monasteries grew up at Clonmacnois in County Offaly and Clonard in County Meath. Derry, Durrow and Kells were linked with the church at Iona. Armagh was another great Christian centre. The Irish monasteries inspired beautiful works of art and craft. In the Book of Kells, produced before AD 800, religious texts are decorated with elaborate patterns, animal designs and pictures.

The Book of Kells may have been produced on the island of Iona, but finished in Ireland.

❋ CAD 650
The *Book of Durrow*, start of
the golden age of Celtic
Christian art

❋ CAD 650
Irish laws begin to be written
down (to AD 750)

❋ AD 697
Synod of Birr discusses
Christian treatment of
women and children

❋ CAD 700
Fine metal working, such as
the Tara brooch and Ardagh
chalice

❋ CAD 800
The *Book of Kells*, the
masterpiece of Celtic
Christian art

31

KINGS, LORDS AND PEASANTS

Irish society was divided into three classes. At the
bottom were the commoners. These included some
slaves, serfs (labourers who were not allowed to leave
the land) and freemen who owned their farms. Life
for poor people was very hard. They lived largely on a
diet of porridge and oatcakes. Hunger and disease
were common. They toiled on the land. Commoners
had to declare their loyalty to the lords and the lords
to the kings. There were many minor kings, but real
power lay with the regional kings of Ulster, Meath,
Munster, Leinster and Connaught. A High King was
based at the ancient royal site of Tara, but rarely ruled
all Ireland because of the endless wars between
Ireland's royal families.

THE VOYAGES OF BRENDAN

Brendan or Brandan was born in
Tralee, in County Kerry, in AD 484.
A Christian saint, he is said to have
founded Clonfert monastery in Galway
in AD 561. Tales about him were
written down later in the Middle Ages,
describing his sea voyages. Brendan
seems to have been a navigator who
sailed the North Atlantic Ocean and
knew its eastern coasts. A description of
the 'mouth of hell' suggests that he may
have seen volcanic eruptions off the
coast of Iceland.

OGHAM SCRIPT

A kind of alphabet made
up of criss-cross lines
was carved on Irish stones
from about AD 300. It is
called ogham. Ogham
fell out of use as
Christian monks in
the 600s and 700s
introduced the letters
of the Roman alphabet.

ⓘ This chalice, a cup used during
Christian worship, was dug up at
Ardagh, in County Limerick, in 1868. It is
one of the finest pieces of metal working
produced in Europe during the early Middle
Ages. It is made of silver and gilt bronze,
with a central stud of rock crystal. It dates
from about AD 700.

❋ AD 577
West Britons defeated by
Wessex at the Battle of
Dyrham

❋ AD 600
Earliest known Welsh poetry,
the *Gododdin*

❋ AD 607
The battle of Chester.
Aefelfrith of Northumbria
defeats the Britons

❋ AD 632
Cadwallon I of Gwynedd
allies with Penda of Mercia to
defeat Northumbria

❋ AD 635
The West Britons start to
call themselves *Cymry*
– the Welsh

THE MAKING · OF WALES

MANY Britons now found themselves ruled by Anglo-Saxons. Others fled westwards. So many sailed off to northwestern France that it later became known as 'Little Britain' or Brittany. Britain itself only became known as 'Great' by way of comparison. After the Battle of Dyrham in AD 577 the Britons of Devon and Cornwall were cut off from those to the north. The last strongholds of the Britons were the Cornish peninsula and the mountainous west, the land that came to be known as Wales.

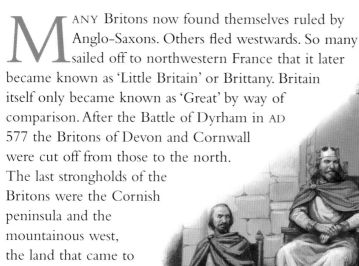

◀ At the courts of the Welsh
kings, harpists praised
rulers for their wisdom and
bravery, or lamented their defeat
by the Anglo-Saxons.

WELSH RULERS

Houses of Gwynedd,
Powys and Dyfed

✤ Rhodri Mawr ('the Great')
AD 844–78
✤ Anarawd AD 878–916
✤ Hywel Dda ('the Good')
AD 915–950
✤ Iago ab Idwal AD 950–979
✤ Hywel ab Ieuaf AD 979–85
✤ Cadwallon II AD 985–986
✤ Maredudd ap Owain
AD 986–999
✤ Cynan ap Hywel
AD 999–1008
✤ Llywelyn ap Seisyll
1018–1023
✤ Iago ap Idwal ap Meurig
1023–39

◀ A great dyke, or
earthwork, was raised
along the Welsh borders by King
Offa of Mercia in about AD 784.
It can still be seen today.

✤ **AD 654**
Last ties broken between the Britons in Wales and the Old North

✤ **AD 784**
Offa's dyke marks the eastern border of Wales

✤ **AD 844**
Rhodri Mawr becomes king of Gwynedd and extends its power

✤ **AD 855**
The royal house of Powys comes to an end

✤ **c AD 945**
The Laws of Hywel Dda are written down

33

THE OLD NORTH

In Welsh history, the lands of the northern Britons are known as the Old North. This region was divided into several kingdoms. They included Elmet (around the hills of the Pennines), Rheged (Cumbria), Manaw Gododdin (around Edinburgh) and the kingdom of Strathclyde. All but the last were invaded by the Angles. An Anglo-Saxon victory at Chester, in AD 615, drove a wedge between Wales and the Old North. Links between the two were finally broken after AD 654.

THE LAWS OF HYWEL

Hywel ap ('son of') Cadell was a grandson of Rhodri Mawr. He came to rule most of Wales and made peace with the Anglo-Saxons. In AD 928 he went on a pilgrimage to Rome. Hywel is famed as a law-maker, for it was in his reign that the ancient laws of Wales were written down. The laws deal with property, murder, theft and the rights of women. They describe compensation for crimes, oath-taking and the part played by witnesses. Welsh law was carried out by trained judges and remained in use for over 500 years. Hywel died in AD 950 and is remembered as Hywel Dda ('the Good').

◀ *Surviving copies of Hywel's laws are in Welsh and Latin, and are illustrated with pictures. They give us a fascinating glimpse of life in the Middle Ages. We learn about farming, fishing, hunting, bee-keeping, about the life of families and communities*

"MEN WENT TO CATRAETH..."

Welsh poetry has a very long history. Some of the earliest and finest verse was written down later in the Middle Ages. The story of the *Gododdin* comes from the Old North and is dated to about AD 600. It describes a British war band which sets out, perhaps from Edinburgh, to attack the Angles at Catraeth (today's Catterick, in Yorkshire). The war band suffers a terrible defeat.

WELSH KINGDOMS

Even when Wales was cut off by the Anglo-Saxons, its merchants and monks could still sail to Ireland, Cornwall, Brittany and beyond. Wales was made up of rival kingdoms. Gwynedd was in North Wales. This kingdom became the most powerful under the rule of Rhodri Mawr ('the Great'), who died in AD 877. In southwest Wales, an area settled by Irish invaders, was the kingdom of Dyfed. It later joined with Ceredigion to make a kingdom called Deheubarth. The royal house of Powys in mid-Wales was said to have been founded by Vortigern. Gwent and other small kingdoms of southeast Wales joined together to form Morgannwg (Glamorgan).

◀ *This tombstone records the death of King Cadfan of Gwynedd in AD 625. The words are written in Latin and his name is made Roman (Catamanus). The words mean 'King Cadfan, wisest and most renowned of all kings'.*

🌸 **AD 597**
Augustine becomes first
Archbishop of Canterbury

🌸 **AD 634**
Oswald becomes king of
Northumbria, introduces
Celtic Christianity

🌸 **AD 664**
Synod of Whitby unites
Roman and Celtic Churches
in England

🌸 **AD 680**
Christian poetry in
English written by
Caedmon at Whitby

🌸 **AD 698**
The *Lindisfarne Gospels*
produced by monks in
Northumbria

THE MAKING OF ENGLAND

ANGLO-SAXON KINGDOMS

Celts

Northumbria — NORTH SEA

Anglo-Saxons

East Anglia

Mercia

Celts

Essex

Kent

Wessex — Sussex

Celts

ENGLISH CHANNEL

A NGLO-SAXON kings such as Offa of Mercia held great power. They constantly attacked neighbouring kingdoms in their search for wealth and more land. Kings demanded personal loyalty and support from their lords, who were called thanes. Many of the peasants were conquered Britons. They included free men called ceorls, as well as serfs and thralls (slaves). Anglo-Saxon merchants traded across the English Channel, the North Sea and the Baltic.

ANGLO-SAXON LIFE

At first the Anglo-Saxons were not great builders of towns, but Canterbury, Southampton, Winchester and York all thrived and the port of London (then in the kingdom of Essex) continued to grow. Some of the land was still covered in thick forest. The sound of axes rang through the trees, as farmers cleared the land for building and ploughing with oxen. They grew peas, beans and barley, wheat or rye. They baked bread and brewed beer. Pigs snuffled under the oak trees, searching for acorns.

🔹 *Kent, Sussex and Essex ruled the southeast. Wessex, in the southwest, grew more and more powerful. Mercia, occupying the English Midlands, was the biggest kingdom. The kingdoms of Deira and Bernicia united as Northumbria, taking in all northern England and Lothian.*

🔹 *An Anglo-Saxon farmstead was surrounded by a few large fields cleared from the forest. Within these, farmers worked their own strips for cultivation and harvest.*

❋ **AD 700**
The Old English poem of
Beowulf is written down

❋ **AD 731**
Bede writes his history of the
English Church

❋ **AD 735**
York becomes an
archbishopric

❋ **AD 757**
Offa makes Mercia the most
powerful Anglo-Saxon kingdom

❋ **AD 798**
Cenwulf of Mercia lays
Kent to waste and tortures
Kentish king

35

BEOWULF AND THE MONSTER

In about AD 700 an exciting tale was told and retold in the halls of the Anglo-Saxon kings. It was written down in the Old English language of the Anglo-Saxons. It took the form of a long poem about a monster called Grendel, which terrorises the Danes until they are saved by a hero called Beowulf. The verse is alliterative, which means that it plays on repeated sounds.

CHRISTIAN ENGLAND

In AD 597 St Augustine and 40 of his monks arrived from Rome with a mission – to convert the Anglo-Saxons to Christianity. King Ethelbert of Kent, who had a Christian wife, became a Christian too. England's first cathedral was built at Canterbury. In Northumbria, however, the Roman teachings clashed with the Celtic version of Christianity, as preached by the monks of Lindisfarne. In AD 664 a meeting or synod was held at Whitby. Here the Celtic Church agreed to recognize the Roman Church.

BEDE'S HISTORY

Bede or Baeda was born in about AD 673 at Monk-wearmouth, in County Durham. He became a monk at Jarrow in AD 703 and studied Latin, Greek, Hebrew, medicine and astronomy. In AD 731 he wrote *The Ecclesiastical* *History of the English People* in Latin. It was translated into Anglo-Saxon and still serves as a very useful guide to early English history. Bede was buried at Jarrow in AD 735 and his remains were later moved to Durham.

As Christians, the Anglo-Saxons built many fine churches of timber and of stone. St Lawrence's is at Bradford-on-Avon in Wiltshire, England. It was first raised by St Adhelm in the 700s, and then re-built later in the Anglo-Saxon period.

❋ **AD 789**
First Viking raids on
southern coast of England

❋ **AD 793**
Vikings attack the monastery
of Lindisfarne

❋ **AD 795**
First Viking raids on Ireland

❋ **AD 795**
First Viking attack on the
monks of Iona

❋ **AD 806**
Vikings kill 68 monks in Iona

SEA WOLVES

IN AD 793 the monastery of Lindisfarne was
ransacked and burnt down. A few years later
the island of Iona came under attack and its
monks were slaughtered. The raiders were
known as Northmen or Danes. They are
often called Vikings, from an Old Norse
word meaning 'sea raiders'. Vikings came
from the lands of Scandinavia – Denmark,
Norway and Sweden. No sight in Europe was
feared more than the sails of their ships coming
over the horizon.

Shields
Shields were round and
made of wood, ringed
with iron or leather. They
were used as a weapon
as well as for defence.

BERSERK!

Viking warriors believed that a heroic death in battle
would bring them glory and a place in Valholl, the
heavenly hall of the Germanic gods whom they still
worshipped. They despised the Christian monks. Vikings were
masters of the surprise attack and raiding from beach or river.
When cornered in a pitched battle, they would form a wall of
shields and fight to the bitter end. Leading warriors would
work themselves up into a frenzied rage before battle. They
were called *berserkir*, or 'bearskin shirts', after their dress.

*Many Vikings spent most of
the year farming and fishing
before joining a war band for the
sea voyage. Some hired themselves
out as mercenaries – soldiers who
fight for a wage.*

Helmets
Helmets were conical and
made of hardened leather
or iron. Some had a bar to
protect the nose.

Weapons
Swords were double-edged in
steel. Many were given pet
names by their owner. The
battle-axe was another favourite
weapon and every ship carried
bundles of spears and arrows.

Battle dress
Most Viking warriors wore simple
tunics, trousers and cloaks. The
wealthier ones wore mail shirts.

❋ AD 838
Vikings ally with Britons in Cornwall, defeated by Egbert of Wessex

❋ AD 839
Vikings kill the king of the Picts

❋ AD 842
Vikings kill people in London and Rochester

❋ AD 850
Vikings start attacking the coasts of Wales

❋ AD 850
Vikings begin to settle in England

37

Wind power
The mast was made of pine. It carried a rectangular sail made of linen or wool.

The prow
The high front of the ship was often finely carved.

The crew
The longship was rowed by 30 or more warriors. They sat on benches or on sea chests containing their weapons, food and cloaks.

Wooden wall
Shields could be slung along the side of the ship as extra protection against enemy arrows.

The keel
The central beam of the ship was made of oak and might be over 18 metres long.

THE VIKING RAIDS

Whalers and seal hunters from Norway had already settled many of the bleak islands to the north and west of Scotland. Norse Vikings came seeking more southerly lands too. Their homeland had barren mountains, forests and cold, dark winters. The milder climate and more fertile lands of the British Isles offered rich prizes. Danish Vikings attacked eastern and southern Britain in search of wealth and adventure. They kidnapped slaves from coastal villages and stole jewellery, silver and gold. They looted the precious chalices, plates and even the bells from churches and monasteries.

The Vikings were expert seafarers. They sailed to war in streamlined wooden vessels called longships.

LANDS IN PERIL

Soon no region of the British Isles was safe from the Vikings. They raided along all English Channel and North Sea coasts. They attacked villages and towns in Wales, Scotland, Ireland and the Isle of Man. They sailed along the costs of Germany, the Netherlands, France and Spain. Vikings travelled east into Russia and down to the Middle East. They sailed west, settling Iceland and Greenland. They even reached North America.

A ship in full sail is shown on this carved stone from Gotland in Sweden. Above it the god Odin rides his eight-legged horse to Valholl.

AD 800
Vikings occupy Orkney and Shetland Isles

AD 830s
Increased Viking raids on Ireland

AD 841
Start of Viking settlement at Dublin

AD 850
Viking settlements on Isle of Man

AD 850
Viking raiders over-winter in England for the first time

JORVIK TO DUBLIN

DURING the 800s, many areas of the British Isles were permanently settled by Vikings. They included the isles of the Shetlands, Orkneys, and Hebrides and the northern and western coasts of the Scottish mainland. They invaded the Isle of Man and occupied the northern Irish coast. After the 830s the Vikings founded settlements at Dublin and other places in southern Ireland, too. Dublin Vikings later married into the royal family of Gwynedd, in North Wales. In England, Vikings captured York, which they called Jorvik, in AD 867. Three years later they invaded East Anglia and killed King Edmund. Their next prize was the Midland kingdom of Mercia.

VIKINGS ON THE MAP

Many place names in the British Isles date from the age of the Vikings. Scandinavian settlements often end in *-by* or *-thorp*. Examples include Duncansby in Scotland or Grimsby and Mablethorpe in England. The ending *-ey* means 'island'. It can be seen in the Channel Islands of Alderney or Guernsey, or in Caldey and Anglesey in Wales. Personal names are also to be found. Knutsford is named after Knut or Cnut.

IN A VIKING TOWN

A typical Viking settlement in the British Isles was built around quays on a coast or river bank. Moored at the jetties there might be a *knarr*, a broad-beamed merchant ship. A small four-oared *færing* might be seen rowing in from a day's fishing, followed by squawking gulls. Buildings were rectangular and normally made of wattle and daub or oak planks. In the northern islands, stone and turf were common building materials.

Inside the home there was a central hearth, hung with cooking pots. There was a loom for weaving and a clutter of barrels and chests used for storage.

❀ **AD 851**
Norwegian and Danish Vikings battle for control of Dublin

❀ **AD 867**
The Vikings take York (Jorvik) which becomes their chief settlement

❀ **AD 914**
New wave of Viking attacks on Ireland

❀ **AD 950**
Death of Erik Bloodaxe, last Viking king of Jorvik (York)

❀ **AD 980**
Christianity begins to spread through Viking homelands

39

◆ The Vikings made fine jewellery, including bracelets, brooches, rings and necklaces.

◆ Fragments of Viking clothing have been discovered by archaeologists at York, including boots, shoes and socks.

Hair
Viking men wore their hair long or tied back.

Plaits and scarves
Women's hair was worn long. It was tidied with a comb made of horn or bone before being plaited or covered by a scarf.

BLACKSMITHS AND WOODCARVERS

Viking settlements included smithies, where sparks flew as the blacksmith forged swords and spears on the anvil and repaired iron tools for the farm. Metalworkers and jewellers produced finer craft, working with gold, silver, pewter (an alloy of lead and tin), with black jet and yellow amber. The Vikings carved wood, stone and whale bone, often using intricate designs of animals. Vikings often formed a business fellowship called a *felag*, which was rather like a company. The members, who might be craft workers, merchants or mercenaries, put up money and shared the risks and the profits of the enterprise.

Dress
Viking women wore a shift of linen or wool covered by a long woollen tunic with shoulder straps fastened by brooches.

Tunic
Men wore a knee-length long-sleeved tunic over trousers. Cloaks would be worn against the cold.

THE TYNWALD

Vikings passed laws and settled disputes at a public assembly called a *Thing*. The Isle of Man assembly met at a grassy mound called the Tynwald. This is still the name of the Manx parliament today. It claims to be the world's oldest legislative (law-making) assembly with an uninterrupted history. Viking assemblies were attended by all free men, but not by women or slaves.

 A Viking chieftain rides to the assembly. Here there would be discussion about new laws and judgements to be passed.

40

✵ **AD 829**
Egbert of Wessex overlord of the Anglo-Saxon kingdoms

✵ **AD 866**
The Grand Army of 'Danes' arrives in England

✵ **AD 871**
Alfred becomes the king of Wessex

✵ **AD 879**
Treaty of Wedmore. Alfred recognizes the Danelaw

✵ **AD 901**
Edward the Elder starts Anglo-Saxon conquest of England

THE DANELAW

NORTH SEA

IRISH SEA

Danes

Anglo-Saxons

Wessex

ENGLISH CHANNEL

DANELAW

THE Scandinavian conquest of East Anglia, Mercia and Northumbria was not carried out by small bands of raiders but by a Grand Army of Danes — an alliance of warriors recruited from many different Viking settlements. Their chief enemy was Wessex, in southern England, for in AD 829 King Egbert of Wessex had become overlord of all the other Anglo-Saxon kingdoms. Now, in AD 871, Egbert's grandson, Alfred, came to the throne. If the Danes conquered Wessex, all England would be in their grasp.

The Vikings' permanent settlements in England were known as the Danelaw. The relentless advance of the 'Danes' was first reversed by Alfred of Wessex.

ALFRED FIGHTS BACK

A great army of Danes descended on Wessex again in the winter of AD 876. Alfred took refuge at Athelney, in the marshes of Somerset. He then fought back and defeated the Danes in AD 878. They gave up the lands of southern Mercia and their leader Guthrum agreed to become a Christian — but Alfred had to recognize the rule of Danelaw to the north.

THE ANGLO-SAXON CHRONICLE

During the reign of Alfred, a history of England since the Roman conquest was written down by Christian monks. The *Anglo-Saxon Chronicle* is not just a record of English history but the record of a language. The writing continued into the 1100s and so it shows how the Old English language developed and changed.

King Alfred is named on this jewelled ornament found at Athelney.

DANEGELD

Shortly after Alfred became king of Wessex, his army was defeated by the Danes. Alfred could think of only one solution — bribery. He paid the Danes money to leave Wessex alone. They did — but only for four years. A later king adopted the same policy. Ethelred II, who came to the throne in AD 978, brought in a tax called Danegeld ('Dane money') to keep the Danes out of the south. Needless to say, they kept coming back for more. The name Ethelred means 'wise counsel' or 'good advice'. He of course became known as 'Redeless' — meaning 'ill-advised'.

In the 700 and 800s, the Anglo-Saxons began to produce large numbers of silver pennies and other coins. Many of these found their way back to Scandinavia. Viking settlements minted their own coinage as well.

❋ AD 926	❋ AD 991	❋ 1009	❋ 1016	❋ 1042	41
Athelstan brings the Britons of Cornwall under Anglo-Saxon rule	Danes win Battle of Maldon. Payment of Danegeld by Ethelred	Vikings under Olaf the Stout pull down London Bridge	Battle of Ashingdon. England under Danish rule	Witan appoints Edward the Confessor as English king	

RULERS OF WESSEX AND ENGLAND
Houses of Cerdic and Denmark

♣ Egbert	AD 802–839	♣ Eadwig	AD 955–959
♣ Ethelwulf	AD 839–855	♣ Edgar	AD 959–975
♣ Ethelbald	AD 855–860	♣ Edward 'the Martyr'	AD 975–978
♣ Ethelbert	AD 860–866	♣ Ethelred II 'the Redeless'	AD 978–1016
♣ Ethelred I	AD 866–871	♣ Edmund 'Ironside'	AD 1016
♣ Alfred	AD 871–899	♣ Cnut I	1016–1035
♣ Edward 'the Elder'	AD 900–924	♣ Harold I 'Harefoot'	1037–1040
♣ Athelstan	AD 924–939	♣ Cnut II 'Harthacnut'	1040–1042
♣ Edmund I	AD 939–946	♣ Edward 'the Confessor'	1042–1066
♣ Eadred	AD 946–955	♣ Harold II	1066

Alfred learned many lessons from the Vikings. One was the importance of ships in warfare. He was the first English ruler to build a fleet. He also reorganized the fyrd, the Anglo-Saxon peasant army.

ALFRED'S LEGACY

Alfred proved to be a wise ruler. He encouraged learning and wrote down the laws of England. In the 890s he planned a new type of stronghold called a *burh* and built many of these to hold back the Danes. His lands grew wealthy from trade. Alfred's daughter Ethelflæd of Mercia fought the Danes in battle and Alfred's good work was continued by his sucessors Edward the Elder, Athelstan and Edgar. However peace broke down after AD979 and Ethelred II provoked a major Danish invasion by the Danish king Svein 'Forkbeard'.

ENGLAND UNITES

After many battles and treaties, in 1016 England came under the rule of Svein's son, Cnut I (Knut or Canute). He married Ethelred II's widow, Emma, and went on to reign over Denmark and parts of Sweden and Norway as well. The appointment of Anglo-Saxon kings had to be approved by a council of nobles, called the Witan. In 1042 the Witan chose Edward, the son of Cnut I and Emma. The ruler of a united England, he was a devout Christian and is remembered in history as 'the Confessor'. He founded Westminster Abbey near the growing city of London.

42

✷ **AD 866**
High King Áed Finnliath drives Vikings from northern coast

✷ **AD 919**
Vikings defeat the Irish at the Battle of Dublin

✷ **AD 951**
Death of Cenéttig, father of Brian Boru

✷ **AD 971**
Brian Boru rules both Munster and Leinster

✷ **AD 999**
Leinster-Viking alliance defeated at battle of Glenn Máma

VIKING TOWNS IN IRELAND

The Vikings' chief town was Dublin, but there were also settlements at Strangford, Carlingford, Limerick, Waterford, Wexford, Cork and Youghal. The Irish Vikings were known as Ostmen ('men from the east').

The Viking hold on Ireland was less complete than that of the English 'Danelaw', being made up of scattered settlements and coastal and river ports.

BLOODSHED AT CLONTARF

T HE Viking attacks on Ireland came in several waves. At first, in the 800s, the Scandinavians – mostly from Norway – came to plunder. Later they built permanent camps and then settlements and towns. The Vikings met fierce resistance from the Irish kings and often from the monks, too. After AD 914 there was another great wave of Viking invasions, and in AD 919 King Niall Glúundúb, along with many lords of Ireland's most powerful family, the Uí Néill, were killed at the Battle of Dublin.

OSTMEN AND IRISH

In these times of trouble, tall, round towers were built at many Irish monasteries, such as Glendalough in the Wicklow mountains. They served as lookouts and shelters against Viking raiders. Sometimes however the invaders joined forces with one Irish king to fight another. The Vikings had great effect on Irish life. They influenced Irish arts and crafts and encouraged long-distance trade. They also taught the Irish their boat-building and sailing skills.

Brian Boru, born in AD 926, was a ruthless fighter who spent as much time battling with other Irish kings as with the Ostmen.

BRIAN BORU, HIGH KING

During the 900s, the royal family of Munster, the Eóganacht, lost pride of place to a dynasty from North Munster, called the Dál Cais. Their king, Cennétig, died in AD 951. One of his sons was called Brian Bóruma, or Boru ('Brian of the Tribute'). By AD 976 Brian had gained control of Munster. By AD 984 he was king of Leinster and by 1002 he ruled all Ireland as High King, going on to conquer the settlements of the Vikings.

❀ **1002**
Brian Boru rules all Ireland as
High King

❀ **1014**
Brian Boru defeats Viking-
Leinster alliance at Clontarf

❀ **1014**
Death of Brian Boru.
Máel Sechnaill II regains
High Kingship

❀ **1014**
End of Viking power in Ireland

❀ **1022**
Power of the Irish High Kings
fragments

43

THE BATTLE OF CLONTARF

The people of Leinster had never been happy with the rule of Brian Boru, and he soon faced revolt on many sides. Brian's son was sent to subdue Leinster in 1013. Leinster allied with the Dublin Vikings and in the spring of 1014 there was a fierce battle at Clontarf, to the northeast of Dublin. The ageing High King's forces won the day, but he was murdered after the battle. Clontarf marked the end of Viking power in Ireland. The *Ostmen* who remained gradually took on Irish ways and language.

This beautiful crozier or staff belonged to the abbot of Clonmacnois in the 1100s. In the century after Clontarf, the powerful Irish Church was reformed by Rome.

IRELAND FRAGMENTS

With the death of Brian Boru, the office of High King passed back to Máel Sechnaill II of the Uí Néill, who had been High King before Brian rose to power. He died in 1022. After that, real power passed back to the kings of the provinces. It was they who laid down the law and taxed the people heavily in order to fight the endless wars they waged upon their rivals.

HIGH KINGS OF IRELAND
House of Niall of the Nine
Hostages (Tara)

✤ Máel Sechnaill I	AD 842–862
✤ Áed Findliath	AD 862–879
✤ Flann Sinna	AD 879–916
✤ Niall Glúundub	AD 916–919
✤ Donnchad Donn	AD 919–944
✤ Congalach Cnogba	AD 944–956
✤ Domnall ua Néill	AD 956–980
✤ Máel Sechnaill II	AD 980–1002
✤ Brian Boru	1002–1014
✤ Máel Sechnaill II	1014–1022

The battle of Clontarf was brutal and bloody, even by the standards of the day.

44

❋ 1018
Battle of Carham. Malcom II
defeats Northumbrians

❋ 1034
Duncan I becomes king
of all Scotland

❋ 1034
British kingdom of Strathclyde
joins Scotland

❋ 1039
Duncan I launches attack on
the English city of Durham

❋ 1040
Macbeth kills Duncan I and
seizes throne

MACBETH'S SCOTLAND

I N 1018 Macolm II, King of Alba, marched southwards
across the River Tweed and defeated the Northumbrians
at the battle of Carham. Lothian was now in Scottish
hands. In 1034 another piece of the jigsaw puzzle fell into
place when King Duncan of Strathclyde, (the kingdom of
the Britons in the southwest) inherited the throne of Alba.
The kingdom of Scotland had now been created and within
it were Scots, Britons and Angles. However Norwegian
Vikings still held on to the northern and western fringes
of the kingdom, and the southern border would be
fought over for hundreds of years.

*Duncan's son Malcolm avenged his
father's murder, killing Macbeth at
Lumphanan in 1057.*

NORSE AND GAELIC

In the Hebrides, the old Gaelic way of
life was now mixed with the Norse.
A group of independent chieftains
arose, part Scots and part Norwegian.
They sailed in longships and answered
to no king. It was not until the 1100s,
when Somerled, ancestor of the
Macdonald clan, gained control of the
islands, that the Viking way of life finally
began to disappear. But even then, the
islanders were a law to themselves.

*The island of Skye is part of Gaelic
Scotland, but the strong Norse
presence there is confirmed by many
place names and by hoards of coins.*

STRUGGLES FOR POWER

The lands of Scotland may have been united under the
rule of Duncan I, but all around the throne there were
old scores to settle and quarrels betwen rival groups or
factions. One faction was led by Macbeth, the
Mórmaer (chief) of Moray who married Gruoch,
granddaughter of Kenneth III. He defeated and killed
Duncan in 1040 and banished Duncan's sons, Malcolm
and Donald Bán, from the kingdom.

DEATH AND REVENGE

The famous play *Macbeth* was written in England by William Shakespeare hundreds of years after the real Macbeth ruled Scotland. In the play, Macbeth is a murderous villain, driven by personal ambition. In reality, Macbeth may have been no more villainous than many other kings of his day. His motives for killing Duncan were probably part of a family feud. Macbeth went on a Christian pilgrimage to Rome and Scotland prospered under his rule. However Duncan's son, Malcolm, supported by his uncle Earl Siward of Northumbria, returned to kill Macbeth in 1057.

MALCOLM CANMORE

Malcolm III came to the Scottish throne in the following year. He was nicknamed Canmore, from the Gaelic *Ceann Mor*, which could mean either 'big head' or 'great chief'! He built a new palace at Dunfermline, which was now the Scottish capital. Malcolm's long reign was marked by endless wars south of the border, with Cnut I and the kings of England that followed him. He was killed at Alnwick in 1093.

RULERS OF ALBA AND SCOTLAND
House of MacAlpin

✤ Kenneth I MacAlpin	AD 843–858
✤ Donald I	AD 858–862
✤ Constantine I	AD 862–877
✤ Aed	AD 877–878
✤ Eochaid and Giric	AD 878–889
✤ Donald II	AD 889–900
✤ Constantine II	AD 900–943
✤ Malcom I	AD 943–954
✤ Indulf	AD 954–962
✤ Dubh	AD 963–966
✤ Culen	AD 966–971
✤ Kenneth II	AD 971–995
✤ Constantine III	AD 995–997
✤ Kenneth III	AD 997–1005
✤ Malcolm II	AD 1005–1034
✤ Duncan I	1034–1040
✤ Macbeth	1040–1057
✤ Lulach	1057–1058
✤ Malcolm III 'Canmore'	1058–1093

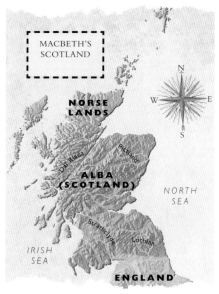

Scotland was fashioned out of four smaller kingdoms Dál Riada, Pictland, Stratchclyde and Lothian. Its southern borders were constantly shifting.

MARGARET, QUEEN AND SAINT

Malcolm Canmore's first wife was Ingiborg, the widow of a powerful Norse leader called Thorfinn, Earl of Orkney. She died and in about 1070 there was another royal wedding, at Dunfermline. The bride was 24 year-old Margaret, daughter of an exiled claimant to the English throne, called Edward the Ætheling. Born in Hungary, Margaret brought the customs of mainland Europe to the Scottish court. Her palace shone with gold and silver, but she was a careful manager of finances. She founded many monasteries and was later made a saint.

Under Margaret's influence, Roman forms of Christian worship replaced traditions of the Celtic Church which had survived in Scotland.

ÏΠDEX

Look up subjects to be found in this book.
Illustrations are shown in *italic* print.

ACKNOWLEDGEMENTS

**The publishers would like to thank the following
sources for the use of their images:**

Page 11 (B/L) Vale of White Horse District Council; 30 (B/R)

British Museum; 20 (B/L) Fishbourne Museum; 28 (B)

Mick Sharp Photography; 32 (B) Robert Estall/Corbis; 33 (B)

Jean Williamson/Mick Sharp Photography; 57 (B)

Ted Spiegel/Corbis; 37 (B/R) Werner Forman/Corbis

All other photographs from MKP Archives

**The publishers would like to thank the artists whose
work appears in this book:**

Julie Banyard, Richard Berridge/SpecsArt, Vanessa Card,

Nicholas Forder, Terry Gabbey/AFA, Sally Holmes,

Richard Hook/Linden Artists, Maltings Partnership,

Janos Marffy, Terry Riley, Martin Sanders, Peter Sarson,

Rob Sheffield, Guy Smith/Mainline,

Rudi Vizi, Mike White/Temple Rogers